Cryptocurrency: Riding the Final Wave!

John Savage

Published by John Savage, 2024.

While every precaution has been taken in the preparation of this book, the publisher assumes no responsibility for errors or omissions, or for damages resulting from the use of the information contained herein.

CRYPTOCURRENCY: RIDING THE FINAL WAVE!

First edition. March 8, 2024.

ISBN: 979-8224318636

Written by John Savage.

I want to say thank you to my lovely wife, Leah, who always supports my endeavors and provides a listening ear, whether it is discussing cryptocurrency, investment opportunities, or how to move my start-up app company forward. Sweetie, I know it can be a lot of information at times but thank you for always believing in me and being there for me. And to my friends and family who always provide support tangibly and through prayer, thank you!

Lastly, to each of my children, Elisha, Miquela, Patience, and Kaylani, thank you for always believing in daddy, helping with my ideas, and testing my apps or helping to create logos.

And most importantly, I thank Yahweh for calling forth what He has put inside of me and for building me up from the inside out!

Cryptocurrency: Riding the Final Wave!

John Savage

Published by John Savage, 2024.

CRYPTOCURRENCY: RIDING THE FINAL WAVE! First edition. March 8, 2024.

ISBN: 979-8224318636

Written by John Savage.

I want to say thank you to my lovely wife, Leah, who always supports my endeavors and provides a listening ear, whether it is discussing cryptocurrency, investment opportunities, or how to move my start-up app company forward. Sweetie, I know it can

be a lot of information at times but thank you for always believing in me and being there for me. And to my friends and family who always provide support tangibly and through prayer, thank you!

Lastly, to each of my children, Elisha, Miquela, Patience, and Kaylani, thank you for always believing in daddy, helping with my ideas, and testing my apps or helping to create logos.

And most importantly, I thank Yahweh for calling forth what He has put inside of me and for building me up from the inside out!

Introduction

What is Blockchain?

What is Cryptocurrency?

Where We Are Headed

Riding the Digital Wave

Stablecoins

Altcoins

Meme Coins

Tokenization

Exchanges

Concerns with CBDC's and FedNow Cold Storage Wallets

Store of Value

What is Utility?

Investing in Precious Metals

The Debt Trap

Wise Money Moves

The Don't Do's of Money

The To Do's of Money

Make Your Money Work for You

CRYPTOCURRENCY: RIDING THE FINAL WAVE!

Having A Purpose

My Top Picks

Real News

Read Between the Lines

Life Does Not Consist in the Abundance of Things

Doing Due Diligence

Financial Tools and Resources

Trusted YouTube Influencers

Only The Beginning

Cryptocurrency: Riding the Final Wave!

Introduction

When I first started out into the world of cryptocurrency, I did not know the difference between blockchain and cryptocurrency. In fact, something about it seemed overwhelming, as if it was something far off and untouchable. At the time I was working on ways to grow my small business and caring for my family. I was a Notary Public providing Mobile Notary services to law firms at the time, continuously looking for ways to sustain and grow my income. Periodically I would hear a brief announcement or conversation in passing about bitcoin or cryptocurrency, but it was just enough in passing to not pique my curiosity.

Later, in the summer of 2017, while in the process of moving to Orangevale, CA my wife and I started looking for a new bed. In 2018 we shopped at Becks Furniture store and decided to buy a bed from them. Over the course of a year after starting a new job as a Financial Counselor, I started developing a report with the Finance Manager there. One day, we got into a conversation about business and during that conversation, he brought up cryptocurrency and told me a story about how his friend told him about Bitcoin and to just put $100 into Bitcoin maybe 3 years prior to that time. He went on about how he thought about it and his friend kept telling him to just invest something into it, but he never did.

He then said, now his friend is doing well and became a millionaire. I mentioned how I had heard of it but knew nothing about it, where to go, or how to even get started. As I left the store, I remained intrigued and began to ponder our conversation and where I could get more information. And in 2019, the following year, I told myself I was going to look into this Bitcoin, cryptocurrency thing and in December of 2019, while on Christmas break from my new job as a Financial Counselor, I

CRYPTOCURRENCY: RIDING THE FINAL WAVE!

locked myself into my room, dug in, and began my search into the world of Bitcoin and cryptocurrency.

When I started the search initially, I was literally clueless and had no point of reference of where I should really start. So, I just went online and started with the questions in my head and the only point of reference I could start with was, "What is Bitcoin"? What is Cryptocurrency? I started with these questions to see what I could find.

As I began my deep dive into the unknown world of Cryptocurrency, to uncover information, I started getting familiar with the term cryptocurrency, blockchain, and identifying exchanges or other places online where I could make my first purchase. As I continued to research and journey into this new world, I began to feel enlightened and a sense of accomplishment.

As 2020 rolled around, I identified two exchanges that seemed legit and where I would not lose any invested funds to the feared, ethereal abyss of the blockchain to nowhere. I came across Binance as my first choice and a short time later, Coinbase, both with offices I identified out of San Francisco, CA. This was a relief because I was living in the Sacramento, CA area at the time.

When getting started, I had to get comfortable first with setting up an account, next getting comfortable with verifying some of my personal information, and then funding my first official transaction into the world of cryptocurrency. I was admittedly a little trepidatious, because I did not want to get scammed and lose my money, or worse, someone trying to commit ID Theft with my personal information. My first transaction was less than $15. In fact, I believe it was $5 dollars.

Everything else up to this point was about testing the process, getting familiar with how things flow, and gaining valuable experience. After a couple months or so, I became more comfortable with the process and how things worked from logging in, how to pick the right coin, to submitting and processing payments within the exchange. In my first few transactions I earned a small fraction of Bitcoin or some other cryptocurrency as I began to successfully explore my way into the world of cryptocurrency. As I continued to do more research to understand what to invest in as a legitimate cryptocurrency, I began learning more about use cases as it pertained to cryptocurrency and blockchain, the technology driving the industry. From there, I began finding various content creators who were sharing their picks, insights, and take on various cryptocurrencies and the blockchain companies behind them.

Some of the crypto influencers I came across were lively, engaging, and provided reliable content they shared with a real desire to teach, educate, and provide continuous updates with all the happenings in the market. They kept things simple enough for me to stay engaged and with enough information to go and do more homework on the cryptocurrencies they highlighted and their current market activities. Some of these crypto influencers include: Meet Kevin, George "We're All George," The Digital Asset Investor, Digital Perspectives, Bearable Bull, and the Crypto Hulk among others. These gave me the insights needed to continue growing and doing my own research online.

There are so many needs that people have and fight to overcome every day. I firmly believe that the blockchain revolution through cryptocurrencies is the gateway to help set many more people free from the mental anguish and bondage that the current fiat system has held over millions and billions of lives across the world, through systems constructed and established long ago. With that said, let's get started as we dive into cryptocurrency and the coming blockchain revolution.

What is Blockchain?

Blockchain is a technology that utilizes advanced computations to track, record, and securely transmit information on what's known as a distributed ledger. The information that is recorded on the ledger is recorded in blocks that have a high level of security known as cryptographic hashes which is where all the details of each transaction is time stamped and recorded on the ledger.

This technology, which is not as new as some people may think, was designed to be faster, more secure, and more economical for organizations to disseminate information and payments which greatly reduce the need for the "middleman" and potential security breaches.

While it is purported that blockchain is designed to be decentralized, to put more control back in the hands of and eliminate expenses for the average business and everyday person, such as you and I, not all blockchains currently and the exchanges they are listed on including, direct websites, are decentralized by any means. This presents the question, who is really in control of and holds your assets?

We will dive into this deeper as we go forward.

(Source Cited: https://en.wikipedia.org/wiki/blockchain) **What is Cryptocurrency?**

Cryptocurrency is an asset built off blockchain technology as a method of transacting business such as payment, recording legal and real estate transactions, sharing gaming units to purchase tools, equipment, weapons, and other items for quest, and a store of value where peer-to-peer purchases can be completed. Simply put, cryptocurrency is a new type of currency that is in digital or virtual form.

The old form of harnessing value in a currency and transacting business has given control into the hands of a few conglomerates and multi-national organizations, and corporations, including the "United States" government. Yes, the is correct, the U.S. government is a separate entity of the American people and has as a result, cost people their livelihood, valuable time with family, increased expenses including increased taxes, online convenience fees, licensing fees, food, gas, oil, you name it.

This new digital wave will allow people from all walks of life to convert their fiat dollars into another form of currency where they don't have to depend on traditional banking systems to store, manage, or distribute their funds or other valuables. The old banking system is antiquated and has been for some time. In fact, it is dead and no longer sustainable now that the entire "United States"economic system is completely indebted and under water.

The Generally Accepted Accounting Principles or GAAP, for so long, has allowed large companies and financial institutions to look more liquid and profitable than they really are. Now, it is time to "pay the piper" who once led a procession of people with sounds of prosperity and ease of financial access with accumulated mounds of debt and debt ridden mortgage instruments with a revolving tax lien attached. This procession led with a calling card that said, "Buy now! Pay later!" Or "this is the American Dream."

The latter part is not really revealed or made transparent until later when people began to realize what they thought was a 6 to 12 month payment plan turned into a 3 -5 year financial noose and bondage. Think car financing, personal loans, etc. Welcome to the new world of origination fees, processing fees, application fees, and compound interest fees (daily).

Simply put, this is another form of OPM or using Other People's Money for other purposes and greater gain. Also, known as passing on all the "cost of doing business" to the consumer. This is why it is so important to read the contract and at the very least, ask very direct and poignant questions when it comes to borrowing money or making purchases you can't really afford. For now, I digress.

Where Are We Headed?

I am still pretty new to the space of cryptocurrency and still have so much to learn about blockchain technology itself and how it is quickly revolutionizing our world, economically, mentally, and ultimately, spiritually. It is up to you to determine what cryptocurrency means to you and what part it will play in your life in the not-so-distant future.

Personally, where I see we are headed is into a One World System or OWS, which is rapidly approaching but still has some time (2030) or sooner, before it is completely implemented and in full effect. Everything in America is inflated, taxes, gas prices, crv taxes, paper shopping bag taxes (CA), disposal taxes, federal taxes, state taxes, import product and excise tax, increasing stamp fees (2024), food prices, and increased medical expenses and insurance costs are up. While prices get higher, some production costs get cheaper and therefore continue to increase profit margins like never before.

This did not just start now, ever since the 1913 institutionalization of Federal Taxation on the average American Citizen (BRIA 11 3 b The Income Tax Amendment), people have been increasingly overburdened with taxes to the point of being taxed out of their businesses, homes, and personal estates in some cases.

In 1970, what was supposed to be one of the greatest rescues of the U.S. banking system, became a step up for more power and ultimately greater control over America's financial future. Negotiating bankers, by force, is what I hardly call a fair and honest negotiation. Nevertheless, the J.P. Morgan Family had a vision of the future and their ability to expand their influence, while helping the American government create a sense of stability and strength.

Where does this position us today? With the fast pace building of blockchain and adoption, we as everyday consumers have an amazing opportunity to get a new fresh start, financially, by becoming our own banks and eliminating the middleman and cutting out unnecessary fees that have continued to plague and diminish the buying power of everyday citizens and their ability to adequately maintain a decent standard of living.

Fortunately, with new technologies and new innovations come new opportunities. With the introduction and rapid global adoption of cryptocurrencies, everyone can now have a say so and can vote with confidence in companies across the crypto sphere who they believe have the everyday consumer's best interest in mind. You can invest your dollars knowing that your consensus matters and literally can change the trajectory and course of a company in real-time. This means, companies are more accountable to you, the consumer, for every single decision they make and how each decision affects the overall markets.

In times of great volatility and instability, there lies great opportunity. Opportunities to solve problems and create viable solutions which spur new growth. Lastly, remember this, more decentralization and less control and influence by large conglomerates and governments also means the people, in mass, have a greater responsibility to come together and unite in our ability to come to a consensus on things that affect our everyday livelihood, and what can be considered a fair and reasonable standard of living.

Riding the Digital Wave

As a society, we have already been on a digital movement and now with the breakthroughs in computational abilities, we are now coming into a full realization of the blockchain wave. The technological advancements that have been discovered and harnessed are nothing short of amazing. One of the greatest values that blockchain is rapidly bringing to market is the hash or mining capabilities of computing transactions which provides greater security the faster computations can be completed on a platform's network.

In today's society, where fraud is on the ramp up and people are concerned about their privacy and financial security, security on the digital networks has now become of greater importance than ever. Blockchain is now providing one of the greatest opportunities in recent history, "for the people and by the people", to take back their finances, privacy, and the way they decide to manage their own personal affairs.

Unfortunately, out of the 86 percent of Americans who say they have heard a little something about cryptocurrency. Out of the 86%, it is estimated that only about 24 percent of the people polled have heard and really know about cryptocurrency, 16 percent out of the 86 percent of this group have experienced using cryptocurrency.

Cryptocurrency is a way to transact and do business on the blockchain much like investing in the stock market by investing an equity stake in a company. The difference is though, buying crypto currency is not considered a security, because there is no purchase of shares in a company or contract with any guarantees. In fact, most of the blockchain organizations out there are currently formed as non-profit organizations.

(www.pewresearch.org/short-reads/2021/11/11/16)

It is important to realize that we are all on the verge of something very revolutionary because it is independent of any single government entity (or at least that is the said intent and purpose by original design) which you have more control over when, where, and how you will spend your "digital dollars" because the fiat system is dead. It is broken, unpredictable, and not backed by anything of real value but has a single point of control, the U.S. Government. This fiat money, from the beginning was designed for ultimate control and subject to manipulation "at will", both from a socioeconomic and geo-political standpoint. Neither of these perspectives are good when you consider all the constituents across the globe it affects.

This is one of the reasons BRICS was formed. For those of you who are not aware, BRICS stands for Brazil, Russia, India, China, and South Africa. And, at the time of this writing, BRICS continues to expand its influence and alliances. The term was first coined back in 2001 by Jim O'Neill who at the time was an economist working for Goldman Sachs. (brics2023.gov.za)

Their alliance and support for each other is to operate independent of the American dollar as the Biden Administration began attacking Russia through "financial War Games" by freezing bank accounts and going after Russian Oligarchs and other resources to stifle their advancement into Ukraine during the war. Of course, there is much more to the story, and we only know in part. This started a long time ago back in 1971 when Nixon, during what's known as the Nixon Shock, rescinded his agreements by taking the U.S. off the gold standard, which was when the real value resided in transacting business and commerce.

This one act gave "the most powerful government in the world", control over Americans' realized store of value and purchasing power. In return, the American public received something fake, an instrument of debt, a piece of paper in and of itself, holds no real value. In other words, Americans, for the first time, as a people, were going to become "borrowers instead of lenders." This also meant, the American people and families would have to "give up" more time with the family to spend more time laboring and working for big corporations and the American Government machine in the years to come.

Fast forward to today, over 50 years later since that time, America is a nation that is to date, in over 34 trillion dollars of debt and counting and a mass of people have become modern day slaves or indentured servants, overcome by mental and emotional stress, more work, and less pay. Food prices continue to increase, gas prices are steadily going up and remain volatile, and taxes remain higher than ever, in fact, the IRS is now

involved in the healthcare system, and has been weaponized in a manner that is keeping many overworked and still underinsured. How does that work? I digress... For now.

In a true, free, and balanced society, it is structured where it is for the people and by the people, not for the government, by the government. This all brings me to my point, it is more important now than ever, for people to learn as much as they can about the rapidly approaching digital age and the global transformation that is already happening, "so you can be prepared, and not scared," as the Economic Ninja would say.

This is why I am writing this book, for people like me who initially knew nothing about blockchain, Bitcoin, Ethereum, cryptocurrency, etc., to educate, enlighten, and encourage anyone who reads this book. You don't have to learn everything about the blockchain industry. In fact, it is impossible to learn everything there is to know about blockchain and cryptocurrencies. I do want to impress upon you, however, that it is going to be vitally important for you to start somewhere and begin learning something.

After December 23, 1913 when President Woodrow Wilson, agreed to a deal to establish the Federal Reserve this began the slow burden and over-taxation of everyday working Americans. Then, in 1971 when Nixon officially removed the American Dollar from being pegged to real assets of gold and silver, to other assets. Bring it to today, we are fastly approaching the "Great Reset" which is prepping us for a one world system and ultimately, a one world government.

Now is the time to work towards getting out of debt and diligently work towards becoming your own bank and take back your financial health. I am not saying you should not keep money at your local credit union or online institution or some other form of custodial care. What I am saying is, it is your responsibility to control your own assets and to diversify what you worked so hard and faithfully to save and accumulate for you and your family, and even your community for those who have a socially responsible organization be it non-profit or for-profit.

Do not trust and depend on the government, institutions, or anyone "single point of failure" that can be easily influenced, confiscated, hacked, or frozen which we actually saw transpire recently with the long-awaited Spot ETF for Bitcoin. This can also happen and could be a real thing potentially in 2024 thanks to the ICE 9 green light going back to a previous administration.

If you would like to learn more about this and many sources in great detail, read, "The Road to Ruin." Let's move on, this part gets deeper than I can keep up with.

Stablecoins

What are stablecoins? Stablecoins are to be looked at as a store of preserving the value of an asset after it has been sold, such as when the dollar prior to 1971 was backed by real gold and silver and could be exchanged at any time by the holder of the receipt or note which was held in a bank.

Simply put, a stablecoin is a cryptocurrency that is often used to hold the value of another crypto asset sold on the open market to protect or preserve value from the major volatility and price fluctuations that can occur. Transferring to a stablecoin can be a great way to protect from any potential tax liabilities in the future until you are ready to cash out or take a portion of your proceeds and put into a new blockchain project or cryptocurrency of choice.

Stablecoins are usually thought of as a safe way to have your money stored without the risk of current bank failure, assets being frozen, stolen, or cash withdrawals being drastically limited at a big bank or other financial institution.

Of course, nothing is without risk of some kind, and this is exactly why blockchain technology has been created, to protect against a single point of failure, mass manipulation, economic instability, or complete government control, that is, unless you decide to buy all into things like world coin, CBDC's, or the massive onboarding of FedNow (coming soon through some economic event or global unrest?! Just a thought). Below is a list of stablecoins currently in the market at the time of this writing:

Tether or USDT has a current market capital of over $83.2 billion dollars with over $83.2 billion coins currently in circulation. Back in 2014 Tether coin USDT was created to facilitate the transfer of fiat dollars into a digital asset.

USD coin or USDC has a current market capital of over $25.7 billion dollars and more than 25.7 billion coins in circulation. USDC is pegged 1:1 to the American dollar and was introduced to the market in September of 2018. Their mantra is "digital money for the digital age."

Dai was introduced to the greater cryptocurrency market in November of 2019 and is an Ethereum built autonomous organization. Dai has a current market capital of over 5.3 billion dollars with a circulating supply of 5.3 billion.

True USD or TUSD has a current market capital of $3.5 billion dollars and a circulating supply of more than $3.5 billion coins in circulation.

On October 7th, 2022, TUSD was authorized by the Commonwealth of Dominica. TUSD became a digital currency "granted statutory status" as a "medium of exchange" and is available on blockchains such as TRON, Avalanche, Polygon, and Fantom to name a few.

BUSD is another stablecoin pegged 1:1 to the American dollar and is issued by Binance, a blockchain company based out of China with

US based operations out of San Francisco, CA. This coin was launched in 2019 on September 5th after approval from the New York State Department of Financial Services in partnership with Paxos, a company that specializes in blockchain.

There are other stablecoins that have now been introduced to the market and for good reason, once America gets "full regulatory clarity", Bitcoin and Ethereum ETFs and others get their official green lights to the market, and crypto adoption becomes more mainstream, money will come flooding into multiple exchanges where billions and trillions of dollars in transactions will happen. Investors, business owners, banks, and people from all walks of life will buy, sell, and hold digital dollars and other altcoins which we will discuss more later. Some of the other stablecoins to check out are USDD, Pax Dollar (USDP), Gemini Dollar (GUSD), Terra Classic (USTC), FRAX, and First Digital USD (FDUSD).

(source: https//coinmarketcap.com/view/stablecoin/) **Altcoins**

Altcoins are all the other currencies created after Bitcoin. They are also known as alternative coins because they provide additional options for investing in and adopting blockchain technologies. Bitcoin is seen as the "flagship coin" or gold standard of digital currency, not because it is the most secure or most efficient because it is not by any means but because it was the first official blockchain introduced and adopted on the marketplace.

The rise of altcoins has brought better, faster, and more efficient means of blockchain technology and cryptocurrencies to the market. This has also caused a significant increase in new millionaires and billionaires with many more people becoming financially independent and economically secure, not to mention debt free.

Many altcoins are a fork from Ethereum or Bitcoin with the majority built off Ethereum, the problem with that is the gas fees are high and not realistic for most people. These are fine if you are financially well off and can afford the cost of the transaction which ends up functioning like a traditional banking institution that likes to charge you fees on your own money which to me, becomes a major price gouge. Also, this can allow the "whales", those who hold millions and billions of a single currency or multiple currencies, to manipulate price and tie up people's money if the platform they are using is not cost efficient. We will go more into this later.

So, what are Altcoins exactly? As referenced earlier, altcoins are any cryptocurrency created after or other than Bitcoin. Bitcoin is considered to be the "flagship" or "Gold Standard" of all cryptocurrencies, which is up for debate based on multiple factors beyond price and limited supply. There are many other blockchains out there that provide a limited number of tokens that provide a greater value, are faster, and more secure, truly decentralized, and can process more information per block at a mere fraction of a cent when compared to Bitcoins high priced, low volume blocks, and not to mention, a high carbon footprint due to the "proof of work" model a.k.a POW.

Below is a list of the top 20 altcoins that have verifiable use cases, high level of security with many interoperable uses and/or unlimited scaling abilities at a fraction of a penny, designed for developers, Dapps, enterprises, and small businesses.

1. ETH (Ethereum) – Many of the other altcoins today are built on the Ethereum network but are extremely costly due to its high gas fees as a result of its Proof-of-Work (POW) modes which requires a lot of power for all the cryptographic proof which also creates a significant carbon footprint. This is one reason alternative altcoins were created, to maximize efficiency,reduce frictions, and widening the playing field for more developers, organizations, and users by drastically lowering fees through these alternative methods. To learn more about Ethereum (ETH), visit www.ethereum.org[1].

Below is a list of the top 10 Altcoins on the market and often talked about on daily crypto news. In a few chapters, I will give my top picks, their fundamentals I have identified, and the value I see them bringing to the broader market long term as the market stabilizes, gains mainstream adoption, and secures regulatory clarity with an unbiased, fair, and transparent regulatory body, especially in America.

XRP – Ripple Foundation – xrpl.org

XLM – Stellar Foundation – stellar.org

ADA – Cardono – Cardono Foundation – cardoon.org

Dogecoin (Doge) – Dogecoin Foundation – created by Billy Markus and Jackson Palmer

Matic (Polygon) – Polygon Labs – polygon.technology Quant (QNT) – Qant Network – quant.network

Algorand (ALGO) – Algorand Foundation – algorand.com Cosmos (Atom) – Interchain – cosmos.network

Binance (BNB) – Binance – bnbchain.org

Solana (SOL) – Solana Foundation – solana.com

Toncoin (TON) – TON Foundation – ton.org

Litecoin (LTC) – Litecoin Foundation – litecoin.org

1. http://www.ethereum.org

Chainlink (LINK) – Chainlink Foundation – chain.link

Currently there are thousands of other altcoins on the market with many more being created daily. In fact, it is estimated that more than 20 thousand coins are currently in existence. Many of them are what I would call a "pump and done" with no real purpose or use case. These coins are often created with the sole purpose of making a quick dollar off the anticipation and excitement of newer and less experienced adopters hoping to find the next 1000x coin that has major pump potential.

Eventually, once we have true regulatory clarity in America, many of these coins are going to quickly go away or subside and cease to exist while the cryptocurrencies with real use cases and problem-solving functions, will be left.

My anticipation is that once this happens and the greater crypto market is consolidated, trillions of dollars will come flooding into the remaining coins and there will be one of the greatest wealth transfers America has ever seen. There will never be another wealth transfer like it again as I do believe we are also nearing the end of an age spiritually and physically.

I say this because control of companies, markets, governments, and systems are being siphoned into a collective few who have confiscated logistical pathways, farmlands, water ways, government positions, legislation through lobbyist, taking over companies, and placing themselves at the head seat of the table by buying up stock in companies for manipulation and voting rights, and more. We will expound upon this more later.

Lastly, many of these coins are also known as meme coins which we will talk about more in this next section.

Meme Coins

By now, with the explosion of social media and the speed at which information, images, and pictures can be shared and disseminated across social media through the mass network of internet and mobile devices, most people have heard of, seen, and even created or shared a meme. By definition, a meme is, according to Merriam-webster.com, "an amusing or interesting item (such as a captioned picture or video) or genre of items that is spread widely online especially through social media. Memes can be funny, satirical, or used as a non-verbal, public display or expression of one's feelings and emotions in response to situations.

Well, the world of the metaverse, cryptocurrency, and NFT (Non-Fungible Tokens) have their own memes introduced on the blockchain. In the crypto world, there are many themed meme coins that have been created to make money quickly through "pump and dump schemes." Coins such as Floki Inu, Obama Harry Potter Coin, Shiba Floki Inu, Shiba Mars, and others, are very volatile and carry a lot of upfront risk associated with them.

Many of these coins have no real use case but can create a few "overnight" millionaires for those who can find them and can get in early before they are found out and are listed on any main exchanges.

Then, there are meme coins that may be considered cute, funny, cool, and in some cases hold real value or use case such as Doge Coin, Shiba Inu,

Pepe Coin, and Wallstreet Meme coin, which is a coin that based on its website, has political and capitalist satire directly associated with it. Even before its major exchange listings which took place in September 2023, it gained thousands of followers. This is also due in part to its marketing efforts.

Memes either have real use cases being created or have a more symbolic meaning behind their creation which has captured the attention of millions of crypto enthusiasts and investors in America and throughout the world. These meme coins have helped to create financial freedom for

many people with an initial investment as little as $100. These can be opportunities, if you find them early and remain patient, reaping huge rewards. Keep in mind though, these are still high risk while at the same time low risk because the initial investment is so small, at least for most people. It's all in perspective and in one's financial situation. Later, we will get more into terminology and actual tools myself and others use to discover these rare gems of opportunity.

Tokenization

Tokenization is the process of replacing sensitive data with unique identification symbols that retain all the essential information about the data without compromising its security. Another way of putting it, in simple terms, tokenization of assets is when you take something of value, sensitive data or information, personal identifiable information including vital stats, legal documents, and real estate and migrate the information on the blockchain, securely protecting the entire essence of the property, image, or data.

Tokenization is a great way to secure personal property in an immutable fashion so it cannot be changed or manipulated in any way. I personally see this as a very effective and efficient way to verify and disseminate information but also a great way to fight against and help prevent money laundering, manipulation of trust documents, and provide a much higher level of ID Theft Protection.

As data breaches, ID Theft, and fraud have been on the rise over the last decade, especially during the pandemic, blockchain development in tokenization has become a greater priority and necessary focus to the greater cryptocurrency industry.

Exchanges

Just as you have exchanges where stocks, ETF's, options, commodities, and derivatives are bought and sold, so it is with blockchain and the cryptocurrency industry. There are a variety of cryptocurrency exchanges around the world where you can purchase cryptocurrencies. In fact, according to Forbes Magazine, there are approximately 1500 cryptocurrency exchanges throughout the world. This is 3 times the number of exchanges that were active in the 1st quarter of 2023.

Similar to buying shares of stock in a company, where you have an equity stake, you are putting dollars into the advancement of blockchain technology. Every dollar invested into a digital asset is a validation, another vote of confidence into the governance, streamlining, and decentralization of the true, unencumbered, Free Enterprise System, "For the People, By the People" free of big government interference or roaming "principalities and powers in high places."

With that said, we know that there are those who will "not let a good opportunity go to waste" when it comes to exploiting the vulnerability and trust of those just coming into the blockchain industry. There have been many actors and Decepticons out there who have set up systems to reward the few to draw the many. This is why I have written this book, so you will not have to start from scratch like I did over the last 3 ½ years. My prayer and hope is that this book will give the right insights, tools, and knowledge to help you make more informed decisions so you are not caught off guard and lose your money like so many others who put most of their eggs in one carton (FTX, Celsius, Voyager, etc.)

Below are some of the largest, most popular, and established exchanges known today:

Coinbase – Centralized

Binance – Centralized

Kraken – Centralized

Crypto.com – Centralized

KuCoin – Centralized

Bistamp – Centralized

Gate.io – Centralized

Binance.us – Centralized

Gemini – Centralized

OKX – Centralized

MEXC – Centralized

PancackSwap – V3 (BSC) – Decentralized

Uniswap – (Ethereum) – Decentralized

Sushiswap – Decentralized

Uphold – (Unique by allowing digital currency's, national currencies, and indirect precious metals investing)

(Sources cited – https:www.coingecko.com/en/exchanges)

There are two main types of cryptocurrency exchanges where you can buy, sell, swap, convert, and send and receive from, Centralized and Decentralized. Centralized exchanges simply means the assets of the user are directly held in custody by the exchange itself which means you as the purchaser of those assets are not in full control of those assets and are vulnerable to hacks, account or asset freezes, or assets otherwise being sold, loaned or subject to other market manipulations by those in control of the exchanges including but not limited to government interference such as Coinbase freezing all transactions of XRP when the SEC went after Ripple Labs and Brad Garlinghouse and Chris Larsen or when Sam Bankman-Fried, Founder and CEO of FTX, who was charged with attempting to commit money laundering, wire fraud, and even breaking

24 JOHN SAVAGE

campaign finance laws using $10 billion dollars of consumer money that was placed in the sole, custody, and care of the FTX Exchange. I will leave this story alone and allow you to do your own due diligence if you want to learn more about what happened.

(Sources cited – nytimes.com/2023/10/04/technology/sam-bankman fried-ftx-trial.html)

Due to the SEC scaling up their attacks on exchanges, in order to intimidate, control, and drain them of their resources through lengthy and frivolous litigation, it is highly suggested that everyone who uses the exchanges, particularly those based in America, to get their assets off the exchanges and to transfer them to a cold storage wallet(s) of your choice.

Now, as you would have guessed, Decentralized exchanges are exchanges where you have direct control over your purchased assets, such as the case with UniSwap and Pancake Swap which make it relatively easy for you to onboard and off board the cryptocurrency assets of your choice because there are no intermediaries that a user needs to go through such as a middleman. This is known as permission-less, a public ledger or blockchain that anyone can be a part of and contribute to.

Concerns with CBDC's and FedNow

First of all, what are CBDC's? CBDC stands for Central Bank Digital Currency or better known as a Fiat currency in digital form. CBDC's are not the "people's money" but the government's money for the purpose of trying to control and maintain their own economic power and to manage the volatility within the economic system.

I personally am not interested in transferring my money and hard-earned assets into any type of CBDC for the following reasons:

• CBDC's are government owned and centralized. This means, if the government in America decides to install a kill switch

because they do not agree with something you say or do, they could essentially cut off or securely limit the use of your own personal funds or access to your assets.

• CBDC's can control and invest your money as they determine best.

• Governments often surveil and track everything because they want to be in the know, they like being in control. This means the CBDC's will become a tracking tool for your whereabouts, movements, and habits.

• CBDC's are controlled by central banks which are basically like a centralized exchange that controls the keys to your assets as long as they are housed on their servers and under their direct custody, care, and control. This is similar to when the Obama Administration gave over the keys to our internet to ICANN, the Internet Corporation for Assigned Names and Numbers.

• Other countries have started implementing the CBDC's and link them to social credit scoring systems. In case you "act up", don't comply, or otherwise fall in line and help maintain the stabilizing of societal norms, you can be penalized, fined, cut off from even basic things such as getting gas, charging your electric vehicle, or buying food.

• CBDC will require you to give up and keep current, your personal information in real-time. Not that a lot of our information has not already been accosted with and without our knowledge. The government will know when you went, where you went, why you went, etc. All your purchases and transactions will be made public on the blockchain similar to now, but it will be more easily accessible in great detail, at no cost, 24/7. This is one way to keep you inline as a proletariat. In other words, your life will become tokenized in real-time so the government can keep track of your every move to keep you in order.

• The CBDC's, I believe, may be a multi-tiered system offering privileges based on your designated status in society. Think matrix, Hunger Games, Divergent, and even, Enemy of The State. Once AI is perfected and successfully integrated into society and everyday life around the globe, I believe it will be the completion of the 2030 Agenda.

• CBDC's in America, will be the driving force behind the FedNow. The government never does anything for free, but it expects you to freely give. When I say it, I am also speaking of "principalities and rulers in high places who expect us to make our life an open book and bow down and ultimately serve the "One World Ruler." I seek to be freely aligned with the pure, unadulterated principles of God in a society where people can be united and free to think for themselves to barter in a form of value and currency of their choosing, without the

interference of an intermediary that only seeks to take away our freedoms and exalt itself above God's economy.

• From my experience, when there is a problem with your bank, when it is a bank error or more specifically, when a governmental agency errors, they make it very difficult to get your money back or access your funds without a lot of proof or access to enough credible information to release your funds back to you. Not in all cases but this can happen so frequently due to not wanting to be accountable and transparent to always do the right thing. To do what is fair, just, and equitable.

• Once your information and paychecks are integrated online with the FedNow, they could program it to take taxes out automatically including social security, state taxes, fines, penalties, etc. without due process or cause and will be empowered to do so even faster than before. This also makes since why there is talk about doing away with having to even report and pay for having your taxes done by a 3rd party in the first place. These are just my observations and what I perceive.

FedNow, is a digital platform created by the Federal Reserve which is not a Federal Government Agency. There are those with authority above most senators and elected officials' security clearance. This is why you had Ross Perot, Ran Paul, Ron Paul, and other elective officials demanding the Federal Reserve open up their books to the public but to no avail, because they do not answer to the public or to the elective officials.

This is why I say do your own diligence when deciding to adopt any digital platform. My question is why does the government need to essentially duplicate a service similar to Paypal, Cash App, Zelle, Square, etc.? Many of the major banks and payment platforms are already on the FedNow platform. This tells me that the government had planned this prior to the pandemic. They never make a move without forecasting and planning ahead the next 10 - 20 years.

When it comes to the future of monetary policy and financial evolution, they are not just planning, they are creating the future.

Banks and other major financial institutions will make it easier for society to migrate right over to the FedNow and other public and private interoperable platforms when the time comes which I believe will start happening between 2023 and through 2024 before things go to the next phase. Not a coincidence it is all being accelerated and taking shape with the rapid sudden approval of Bitcoin and Ethereum ETF's right in the progression of the greatest and most volatile election year America will ever experience again.

Cold Storage Wallets

A Cold Storage or Hard Wallet is when you hold your personal crypto and blockchain assets on a device that is in your sole custody, care, and control. This means essentially you have removed the middleman (banking institutions) from intercepting and processing your transactions and you have now become your own bank. No other exchange, whether centralized or decentralized, has access to or control over your digital assets. This is very important for many obvious reasons such as:

- There is no one holding any funds in excess of $2000 that needs to wait to settle.

- No fees to cash a check.

• No issues being judged because you come into the bank looking rough in your gym clothes and you are told you cannot cash your own $100k bonus check from a major fight you won, which happened by the way. Imagine that your own institution where you bank and help keep people employed, tells you to go away, they refuse to allow you to cash in on your own hard earned money.

• No issues with missing funds from your bank account because of some banking software issues and having to fight to get your money from the bank that could very well be underfunded but you never know. This situation too happened to more than one person I provided financial counseling too.

• You're protected against hacking, cyber-attacks, and bank failures.

• No wire transfer fees.

Cold Storage Wallets are like regular wallets or mini vaults you can load on to any mobile device. You can also purchase a Hard Wallet that you can carry with you as a stand-alone mobile device or in card form that goes into your actual purse or wallet. Below is a list of some of the most popular and time-tested Cold Storage Wallets on the market today.

These are in no particular order and as always, do your own due diligence on which devices meet your needs best and suit your desires based on cost, design, functionality, user interface, ease of use, capacity, etc.

Tangem Wallet

The Tangem Wallet is easy to use and set up. It only takes a few minutes and requires you to download a mobile app on your mobile device so you can visually check, manage, and convert balances.

- It is in the form of a card that is of high-grade material that is super durable and highly effective against wear, tare, temporal elements, and abuse.

- It's the size of a credit card so you can take with you anywhere you go.

- It is discreet.

- It takes less than 5 minutes to set up.

• Has not been hacked since its inception in 2018.

- Has a 25-year warranty.

- Has a high military grade security EAL 6+ (Evaluation Assurance Level) which means it has been functionally tested against security threats to ensure your assets are protected and always kept private.

- One of the best wallets on the market at a very affordable price starting around $45 and up.

- Protected against wear and tear including extreme hot and cold temperatures.

- Solid company with many big-name partnerships including Wallet Connect, Stellar Foundation, Cardano, New Balance, GBBC (Global Blockchain Business Counsel) and Draper Associates.

(Sources Cited – htps://tangem.com/en/)

30 JOHN SAVAGE

Ledger

Ledger is another Hard wallet that offers a list of devices to choose from. It has had a few hacking attempts with a couple being successful to a degree where some holders wallets were affected including at the end of 2023. Their team is responsive and quickly worked to identify and secure the vulnerability they found during a software upgrade.

• Ledger is still widely used and trusted but should never be used as your sole source for storing your prized assets on a Cold or Hard Storage device.

• Easily portable and requires USB-C connectors to check and view assets including a secure key to load and off load your assets.

• Accepts Ethereum and Polygon NFTs.

- **Can connect 3rd party wallets to accept over 5000**

cryptocurrencies including Multi-Blockchain NFT's. This one significant reason for many uses continuing to use this

technology since it can accept more cryptocurrencies allowing you to move them around securely and quickly from one source to another as necessary.

- It is compatible with Android, Apple, and Linux devices and Windows.

- Asset recovery phrase and CC EAL5+ protection.

- The Ledger device prices range from $89 - $318.

- It takes a few minutes to set up and get used to, and it has a limited number of cryptocurrencies you can load based on the device you decide to purchase due to storage capacity. This is why some people may have several Ledger Wallets.

- It is a very popular product and promoted and used by many of the industry's top social media influencers.

- The devices also come in an array of colors.

NGrave

The NGrave Wallet has been around for more than 5 years and considered to be the "Gold Standard" when it comes to the top cold wallets out on the market today. In fact, medium.com wrote an article calling the NGrave Wallet the "coldest of all cold storage wallets."

• Everything is completely offline.

• It currently has the highest level of security. It boast a EAL7 Certified operating system see

https://www.ngrave./o/?sca_ref=1739249.ya6SMzzdU)   •
Has a vibrant color display screen to view and manage all of your crypto assets securely.

• The company's advisor, Jean-Jacques Quisquater was referenced in 2009 Bitcoin paper by Satoshi Nakamoto for his early contributions to Blockchain.

• Your wallet is synced using a QR code, concealing your private keys.

• Use the easily viewable display to verify and complete your transactions.

• See everything in real-time.

• "On and off ramp" coins, ETH, and Multiverse tokens. • Depending on the product you purchase, prices currently range between $398 - $498. Pricey but well worth the quality and security if you hold a significant number of high value assets.

Treazor

Treazor is another widely popular Hard wallet to securely store all your crypto and NFT assets.

• Treazor has a small digital display with 2 buttons to navigate your transactions on the model 1 and the Treazor Model T which has a slightly bigger touchscreen display.

• Has widely been used and trusted by many of the top cryptocurrency enthusiasts and influencers.

• Now comes in multiple colors.

• It boasts a high level of military grade EAL6+ chip. • It can confirm every transaction directly on the app. • Uses tor privacy software to help protect your identity. • It is the first to implement the SLIP-0039 Shamir security

standard (your 24-word seed phrase is secured among multiple locations)

• The Treazor withstand extreme temperatures from -20 degrees Celsius to 140 Fahrenheit.

SafePal S1

The SafePal has a simple sleek design that makes it easy to handle and use. It is one of the top Cold Storage Wallets used to secure your valuable crypto assets.

• The screen and app are visually appealing and intuitive. • Offers a great level of security at a very affordable price. • Supports over 19 blockchains and thousands of cryptocurrency projects.

- **Integrates Binance for easy spot trading, bridging, and cross chain swapping all within the security of the wallet.**

  - Track the cryptocurrency market within the wallet in real-time. • Stake and avoid gas fees.

  - For the starting price of $49, the SafePal S1 Cold Wallet includes many great features like NFT's, imparting external wallets, mnemonic phrases, and more.

- 1-year warranty with 24 hour support.

BitBox02

BitBox2 is another Cold Storage option that features one of the most compact designs on the market today. It has hundreds of views on Trustpilot with an average score of 4.9.

  - BitBox02 is mobile and easily concealable. Looks like a mini-USB device.

  - Swiss Made.

  - Open-Source code which means anyone can view and verify transactions.

  - The private keys are stored offline.

  - Supports over 1500 cryptocurrencies.

  - Offers U2F authentications (Universal Second Factor Authentication).

- When compared to the Ledger Nano X and Trezor Model T, the BitBox02 offers additional security and additional back-up features.

To conclude, these are just a few of the most secure and widely trusted Cold Storage wallets used on the market today. Some of the other cold storage wallets out there include Arculus, KeepKey, Blockstone, and Kestone. Whichever Cold Storage Wallet you choose, make sure to do your research into the one that fits your price range, security needs, quality, user friendliness, etc.

Also, keep in mind, each company will have more than one option in terms of wallets and even additional auxiliary products to choose from. No matter which wallet you choose, remember to secure your keys and passphrases, and keep your assets off the main exchanges. To learn more about each device, their features, security breaches, or concerns, even just how to use your device, go online to their websites and check out YouTube videos by many of the influencers and company representatives themselves to get started.

Store of Value

So far, we have talked a lot about cryptocurrency and the monetary system. Now, let's talk about a store of value and what it means. A store of value is a method by which you take something of value to you and transfer or repackage it in a manner where the value of the specific asset you hold is stored in a form by which you can preserve and protect it from loss and to protect its value from being diminished over time due to external variables such as rising cost, inflation, or by some other means of manipulation and volatility which that asset could realize a reduction in future purchasing power such as systemic instability and geo-political conflicts.

Below are some examples of viable stores of value:

- Putting money into a high yield savings account.

- Placing funds inherited into a 3- or 5-month treasury bond until you have found a meaningful way to properly divest the funds.

- Moving money from a no interest savings account into gold, silver, palladium, etc. as a guaranteed way to preserve value and hedge against future inflation, wars, and a destabilizing country.

- Investing in blue chip stocks that yield dividends and have an established history of being stable and realizing profit and growth during times of great economic volatility and even war. Specifically, investing in companies that always paid out dividends on a monthly, quarterly, and annual basis.

Simply put, a store of value is anything you transfer value to in order to preserve the value of that asset or commodities to maintain its current and future purchasing power which also depends on what medium of exchange you use to hold, store, or transfer the value of those particular assets.

Cars, paintings, livestock, wines, homes, are all forms of some store of value which are regularly found among individuals of high net worth who I would consider savvy investors many times. But, for the sake of the current subject matter, we will stay focused on cryptocurrencies as the main medium of exchange by which we transfer, secure, and privatize assets in this rapidly evolving digital age.

Today we have even more options and ways of storing the value of an asset by way of blockchain technology. Cryptocurrencies are simply a means by which we can securely transact business and the essence of what is valuable to use to protect it against theft, loss, water, fire, or other elemental exposures including basic human error or hacks.

Before choosing a particular store of value, consider your knowledge, experience, and risk tolerance or appetite for accepting a particular risk. Because everything has some level of risk present with red flags everywhere. Currently, there is more risk within the cryptocurrency markets due to the industry being relatively new, rapidly expanding, and becoming a globalized machine that is for all intents and purposes, in 1st gear. As we quickly realize the demise of the once mighty dollar as a mere shell of what was the world's reserve currency, we are now approaching 2nd gear. Fast forward, as we transition to a new digital economy, blockchain is completely transitioning the world into a globally digitized world where paper currency or fiat are losing their chains on the masses and will be soon declared useless.

Blockchain technology has now evolved to where legal and real estate contracts have been and are being digitized on the blockchain networks so no one can manipulate records, transfer property, or forge information from one party to another without the rightful owner's knowledge. Smart contracts are contracts built on the blockchain that was created using computer coding with the terms, information, and any set conditions by which the contracts on the blockchain are executed.

Just like "offer and acceptance" for the terms of a contract to be accepted between two parties must be met. Once the agreement or programmatic conditions are met, the contract can be successfully executed.

Some of the top blockchains that currently deploy smart contracts include Ethereum where most of the many altcoins are built on or on top of which is one reason with Ethereum being one of the first chains to be widely used, has such high gas fees, making it very costly to use. Stellar (XLM) which is super-fast and cheap to send funds across, Cardano (ADA) which has a partnership the school systems in Ethiopia to help track a list of educators and students, Solana (SOL) which is "resistant to censorship", is fast and secure, Polkadot (DOT) which acts as a "unique digital fingerprint" for documents stored using its blockchain.

(https://www.trustradius.com/smart-contracts)

I believe that smart contracts are going to be a more efficient and cost effective way to secure, transact, and process business in less time which in the long-term should equate to lower accounts receivables, a greater number of client accounts being processed and closed out each month, a smaller number of security breaches, lower overhead, and operational cost, and increased net revenues with higher profit margins.

What Is Utility?

Utility refers to a particular token built on a specific blockchain utility or a specific purpose of use. Every blockchain is built with its own use case and allows the user to support the work of that blockchain. Another way to look at utility is a particular ecosystem's functionality for which it was built, such as interoperability between banking rails like JP Morgan and Blackrock, to send sizable financial transactions seamlessly between banks, uber fast and cheap.

The metaverse is another ecosystem built on ERC-20, Ethereum Blockchain, designed to allow gamers and developers around the world the ability to create new, real like, virtual worlds to connect players around the world, giving them the ability to create and sell equipment, weapons, avatars, and new playing experiences in real time. Players can also earn real tokens on these platforms as an incentive to try out the platforms and virtual worlds as a means for generating mainstream adoption.

There are many other cryptocurrencies as alluded to earlier that have no real utility or purpose other than to scheme and create a pump and dump experience for the creator of that token. Rest assured, the time is fast approaching where these "bad actors" are being flushed out by their own demise, the SEC crack downs (Where it really counts) and the over exposure of the greater cryptocurrency community. My simple take on utility is this, whatever industry, or token you have an interest in and may even be connected to where you are knowledgeable, start there and do your own research before advocating for or investing your hard-earned dollars.

Know what you're doing and why you're doing it, and make sure you only use funds in your budget that you are able and willing to lose or weather the volatility of the market with.

Investing In Precious Metals

Investing in precious metals is something that is out of touch for many people and it has never crossed their mind, not because they are not capable or can't afford it, but because our system has been built on a house of cards to keep people in debt. Our forced dependency on a currency that lacks in real backing of value behind it, fiat system has caused and was designed for people to become indebted to it as indentured or bond servants. I digress for now but will share more on this later.

Precious metals have great intrinsic properties. Adonai created the foundations of the world. Paper money is simply an instrument of debt with the "Promise to Pay", backed by the "full faith" in a governmental system who uses it to establish it to secure, and control a society and the constituents that side in the construct it is created. As long as people buy into that construct or system and there remains perceived value, the "fiats" will continue to be used and people will remain manipulated, controlled, and influenced by that system right down to their habits, behaviors, and ultimately belief systems. This system has remained a well-oiled engine as long as it has due to the psychology behind marketing, sales, and advertising.

On the other hand, when it comes to precious metals, which is "God's" money, that's not just in quotes but it is emphatic truth. All the metals and precious metals have and always will retain great value, purpose, and use case as long as the earth remains, which is why it is important to learn more about how to research, buy, and hold some bullions on your persons, in a vault, and/or a custodian of your choice. Consider some of the reasons to hold metals such as Gold Silver, Palladium, Platinum, Rhodium, and more:

Gold

- It has been used throughout history as a proven means to barter and will not biodegrade or rot away because it can maintain its molecular properties in various elements and conditions.

- It is great for use as jewelry that's why people spend fiat for it essentially creating value out of something that has no value. You can wear it, sell it, and trade it at will.

- You can barter with Gold with nearly anyone who understands its value.

• It has value in abundant times and lien times because it can be

CRYPTOCURRENCY: RIDING THE FINAL WAVE! 39

used to serve multi-functional purposes.

• Gold is a great hedge against inflation and can be a stabilizing medium of exchange when an economy such as a superpower like America once was, crashes.

• Gold is considered the most widely utilized of all the precious metals found on earth due to the unique structure of its properties.

• Gold is an excellent conductor that is used in cooking instruments, phones for its ability to transmit signals, candy wrappings, many electronics used today, jewelry, clothing, buildings, and more.

• It has many healing properties as well to help improve circulation in the body.

As of 2022, the following countries in order are holding vast amounts of Gold and producing metric tons of gold each year:

1. China – 368.3 metric tons

2. Russia – 331.1 metric tons

3. Austria – 327.8 metric tons

4. America – 190.2 metric tons

5. Canada – 170.6 metric tons

6. Ghana – 138.7 metric tons

7. Brazil – 107.0 metric tons

8. Uzbekistan – 101.6 metric tons

9. Mexico – 101.6 metric tons

10. Indonesia – 100.9 metric tons

This list is according to Forbes Magazine, who is well known for tracking wealth, business, and all things money.

(Sources cited – https://forbes.com/sites/greatspeculations/2021/06/23/updated-top-10-gold-producing-countries/?sh=3ffd3cd52ce2)

According to Geology.com, the top 19 producing along with all the other Gold producing countries, as of 2022, produced more than 3200 metric tons of Gold. If there is no real value in holding Gold as a viable form of currency, instead of paper dollars which cost more resources to produce it than it is worth, then why are so many countries harvesting it daily. According to an article written by Market Watch on October 8th, 2013, there was a 10 percent increase in production cost for every $100 dollar bill produced from 7.8 cents to 12.5 cents. So, for every $100 dollar bill produced, there was a debt obligation attached to it. Instead of receiving a $100 dollar bill that was worth $100 1:1, it had a net retained value of $99.87.5 cents attached to it.

Another way of saying this is the American government or any government for that matter does nothing for free. They will always find a way to recoup costs by means of taxes, fees, inflation, regulation, confiscation, etc. So, just know when you go to the store with a $100 bill, it is less than the actual face value stated and before you get paid from a regular W-2/4, consider that, every American is taxed about 30 percent minimum of their income which includes FICA, S.S., State Disability (EDD), State Taxes for states that have state taxes, etc.

Let's look just a little further at the stronghold or accosting of our purchasing power when tied to a federal government backed anything. Take $100 -12.5 cents in Private (Federal) Production cost = $99.875 dollars x .30 percent in employee taxes = $29.9625 dollars in total taxes taken for every $100 dollars earned. Keep in mind, this all happens before you receive your check and still have to pay your utility bills, house note or rent, car note, gas for your vehicle, or purchase groceries for your family.

So, this number in my calculations comes to $100 dollars or for every $100 dollars earned, the average American tied and completely dependent upon the "Fiat ", is actually taking home approximately

$70.0375 or roughly 70 percent of every dollar earned. This means, for the average, hardworking American paying 50 percent of their gross income towards household expenses, they in fact have around 20 percent of the income left or less than 30 percent of net take home pay left to live on.

You may be asking, how is that even possible? It's not! It's not even practical to ask the average American to have to pay those kinds of expenses. That is exactly why, a lot of people I have met over the years, have retired or left America for another country with less expense and where their dollars will go 3-5 farther on less.

The whole point is, this is why we need to invest our dollars or transfer the true value of our time into a vehicle or asset(s) that will better shield us from an economic system that is designed to confiscate the value of our efforts through everyday transactions which are maintained by us but not for us. We need to preserve the value of what we work for by levering our time and energy into more stable and guaranteed methods and strategies that can and will repeatedly yield returns for us that are profitable on a weekly, monthly, quarterly, and annual basis.

This is where transferring the value of your currency from "fiat" holdings to precious metals and digital currency and its future is more important now, than ever in the history of America and the world.

Here are some of the other precious metals and their uses and value they hold. In fact, metals will be and are starting to be pegged to certain cryptocurrencies on the blockchain:

Silver

- Carries healing properties similar to gold.

- Used for jewelry by most consumers around the world. • It was once regularly used as a eating utensils or "silver ware",

42 JOHN SAVAGE

hence the name.

- It's used in capturing images and producing photo images "due to silver bromide (silver and bromide cubicle crystal structures) and iodides sensitivity to light."

- Silver is used in electronics as well. See (https://www.rsc.org/ periodic-table/elements/47/silver)

• It is used as a reflector in clothing and mirrors.

• Silver has anti-fungal/antibacterial properties which is excellent for eliminating or reducing the accumulation of bacteria on the feet and clothing. This is especially great for athletes or those who must walk long distances a lot.

• It is also used to purify water and as silver nitrate in some mouth washes and toothpaste.

• Over 20 tons of silver is produced each year.

• It is malleable and easy to work with unlike other common metals used like copper and nickel.

Palladium

• Number 46 on the periodic table of elements, Palladium is a shiny metal that looks similar to silver. Palladium gets its name from Pallas, an asteroid. The metal has many industrial uses and I see its demand and increased production on the horizon as the research and demand for electric vehicles as well as the advancement in fuel cells increase. It is a rare earth metal that is grouped with other platinum metals including iridium, platinum, and rhodium.

Sources Cited (https://ww.investopdeia.com/terms/p/palladium.asp)

Palladium is currently priced around $1108 and can be tracked daily at kitco.com which tracks commodities in the precious metals sector. This metal is 30 times rarer than gold and at one point it was priced higher than an ounce of gold at more than $2900 per ounce.

Below are some of the uses of Palladium and why it holds such value:

• As with other rare metals, it is used to make jewelry. • It is a great catalyst in catalytic converters by breaking down harmful chemicals from vehicle emissions.

• Palladium is regularly used in dental fillings.

• It is also used in fuel cells and as the demand for fuel cells grows, the demand for palladium will grow also.

• Palladium is even used in mobile cell phone production. • War components and nuclear fusion (a process by which energy between atomic nuclei such as deuterium and tritium (used in gun sights) is harnessed and used for a reliable source of energy).

Simply put, Palladium along with other rare earth metals will eventually be tracked and transacted for their value on the blockchain if it has not already started. And it is also a great source or alternative for transferring and storing value because of its rarity, variety, and usage.

The Debt Trap

Just like with all opportunities to grow, invest, preserve, and source your income, make sure you consider the risk and evaluate your level of understanding. This is important because many people found themselves overleveraged and putting all their crypto up for security as a hedge of what they thought may happen in the economy, stock market news, and with hopes of riding the overpriced tokens in the market to even higher highs.

I have been learning being newer to the space, you must understand the volatility and manipulation that can and still does happen in the

cryptocurrency market, which can cause you to lose your entire portfolio value if you're not careful. A lot of investing across the markets can be very emotional, sometimes because of greed and with others, the real hope of getting out of debt and freeing themselves from an oppressive and antiquated system.

Being anxious and overly excited has caused many people to take out loans, invest more than they can afford, and even put up their most precious assets as security to place large orders on margin. There are people who found themselves in greater debt and having lost everything because they did not understand the markets or what they were getting themselves into.

Never invest what you are not willing to lose and definitely stay away from margin calls. When that money is called and you do not have the money you expected, you're in trouble. It is like getting a payday loan for $2000 to cover your house note and you think you will have the $250 to start making the payment next month only to find out the $250 loan payment you planned for has now ballooned beyond your budget to $500 per month due to the origination fees, application fees, processing fees, and interest rate being tacked on top of that.

As a Financial Counselor, I have talked to people every day who tell me how they had money but due to an emergency, they can't pay back what they owe or the amount they have to pay back is beyond what they initially budgeted for. This is due to the power of compound interest on steroids working against people.

I always like to encourage people I work with whether they are making $25k a year or $300k a year, to start small if you must and work your way up over time. It's less invasive to your current financial state and easier to control the outflow, especially when working with a plan to get out of debt.

Nothing great happens overnight, regardless of what you may hear.

Below are some tips for avoiding the debt trap that I have learned:

- Never borrow money to invest.

- Never hold on to all your profits, especially in one place such as the open exchanges where some people have been hacked or suffered loss due to a down market.

- Never put your investments on margin unless you really know what you are doing. If the margin is called and your investment has gone the opposite direction, payment will be due

immediately. This is where you would need to put a stop loss trigger in if you know what to do.

- Never take out a personal or payday loan to invest your money. • Research your investment choices before you decide to place your funds.

- Take your time and don't rush to make money, that's when you're likely to make a poor decision and it can actually cost you more in the long run than what you started with.

Lastly, make sure you have a basic budget set up to help you track your monthly inflows and outflows and to help you manage what you can reasonably invest each month.

Wise Money Moves

Tracking savings and managing your money is a lifelong journey. It takes discipline, practice, learning, and organization of methods to know what works or does not work for you personally. There are many things to consider when exploring ways for you to earn an income, how to invest funds properly, and grow your money. It takes a lot of patience, a clear strategy, and controlling your emotions when it comes to ebbs and flows of money setbacks you may face. This is why it is so important to have understanding and to know what type of investor you are and your own personal relationship with money.

We all have different levels of understanding about money and finances based on what we have learned, what we have been taught, and ultimately what we have been exposed to early in life, which influences our personal relationship with money. There are many things I have had to learn when it comes to my own relationship with money, including what risk is a good risk, when opportunities may seem better than another but ultimately is a complete waste of your time in the long run (distractions).

You must focus more on things that cater to more of your skills and giftedness, as well as your own values, goals, and temperament. Another thing that is very important to consider is relationships in money. Sometimes one spouse is more risk averse, and another is more calculated and willing to take risks that make sense and can be controlled.

With that said, let's look at some dos and don'ts of wise money moves and how you should better manage your dollars for a secure financial future.

The Don't Dos of Money

- Don't borrow to invest.

- Don't invest in high-risk investments without understanding the risk involved and having a solid stop loss/ exit strategy. • Don't borrow more than you can afford or willing to lose and can pay back with reserves.

- Don't invest with the expectation of getting rich or turning a profit quickly.

- Don't invest your money without a backup plan or

contingencies in place.

• Don't invest without a purpose or goal in mind for that particular investment.

• Never leverage all your assets such as a car, retirement account,

or home to invest in a high-risk opportunity. This includes savings accounts.

• Don't invest unless you have a genuine knowledge or interest for the company or industry for which you are desiring to invest.

• Don't depend on someone else to understand and manage your investments for you. A lot of professional athletes and

entertainers have been drained of their accounts over time or paid way too much to have someone with a lack of character or greed to oversee their financial affairs. That is why many have gone broke or have only a fraction of what they earned over time.

• Don't invest without budgeting for it each month.

The To Do's of Money

- Always have a purpose and plan for every investment you make.

- Set a clear budget for what you are going to save and invest each month.

- Do some research on different strategies and find the methods that work best for you.

- Always have an exit strategy.

- Decide which investments will be short-term (less than 12 months) and which investments will be long-term (held for more than 12 months; ideally up to 10 years).

- Find out whether you are a conservative investor, moderate investor, or an aggressive (high risk investor). Knowing this will help you determine the type of investment vehicles and strategies that best fit your money personality.

- Find what works for you and four goals and then stick to it while making slight adjustments over time.

- Do make sure you take some profits on shorter term investments and consider holding some profits in a (Money Market Accounts) if you have one available. This will create an additional source of funds to access if you come across a great opportunity to swoop up such as stocks, options, cryptocurrency, or other investment opportunities.

• Consider cryptocurrencies, exchanges platforms, and other opportunities to yield consistent returns or other dividends, in some cases, you can earn free crypto currencies through opening a new account, completing task, and watching learning videos, such as the case with Coinbase, Crypto.com, Webull, and Robinhood, just to name a few.

No matter where you decide to place your funds or other assets, regardless of if it is directly with a crypto exchange, Bitcoin ETF through a brokerage firm such as Fidelity or JP Morgan, make sure you find out what that platform offers in terms of tools, strategies, education, notifications, and more importantly, stability and ease of use.

Find a mobile or online platform to connect with, that you find intuitive and formattable to use, and transact business on. The last thing you want to do is lose your finds or tokens or pay astronomical fees for a transaction that was supposed to be at a low transaction fee because you accidentally executed a transaction at a Market Rate instead of Limit Order or high gas fees on the ETH network. The Ethereum network can be super expensive at times and gas fees have only increased as demand, usage, and prices have increased.

Make Your Money Work for You

Before you can make your money work for you, it is important to create a budget and to know where your money is currently going. It does not matter if you have a lot of money or enough to cover all your bills with a little extra, the first goal should be to identify if you are in the red or in the black each month. If you see you are in the black each month and you have enough money left over each month to get your dollars working for you, great. If on the other hand, you find yourself in the red each month, then it is important to know by how much you are in the red to see if there expenses you can eliminate or cost you can cut out to save money and reallocate those funds to either a high yield savings account or dollar cost average in some type of stable investment vehicle until you can start increasing your investment holdings.

I recognize for the majority of Americans at this time, it is not as easy or linear to make the adjustments, especially in light of the failing dollar, in a country that is structured for and built off indebtedness, undue taxes, and "convenience" and processing fees everywhere. But you and I and every great, hard working American, especially the "middle class", are not victims and are empowered to overcome any challenges we may be facing or setbacks we have experienced.

God has given every man and woman a measure of faith and it is this faith that each of us has been endowed with to overcome life's greatest challenges, delays, and setbacks, including finances. In fact, if there is ever a time for all of us to truly break free financially and walk in true financial liberation, Now Is That Time!!! In times where things seem the darkest, is where opportunities light up the brightest. As America now comes face-to-face with its greatest economic uncertainty in the nation's 247-year history it is time for us to be in charge of our own financial health like never before.

We must dig in, get focused, get help if you need it, and there is lots of help, support, and resources online today with many of today's social media influencers, commentators, and educators, who I strongly believe, have been placed by God Himself for such a time as this. Not just in America, but around the entire world, to set people free from financial bondage and in some cases oppression, to live a life of thriving and not just surviving.

Proverbs 6:5 says, "Free yourself, like a gazelle from the hand of the hunter, like a bird from the snare of the fowler." Often it becomes a fight once we find ourselves paying out money faster than we are bringing it in but that is where we must look outside ourselves and our situation for resources and mentors to help us get free and then the disciplined practices to stay focused. Our time is one of the greatest assets we have on this earth in addition to our faith, which is what we exercise to walk in freedom and financial independence.

Proverbs 22:7 says, "The rich ruleth over the poor, and the borrower is servant to the lender." These two versus I just shared are what I hold dear to help me keep moving forward at times to remind me and encourage me to not give up as I diligently work towards financial freedom so I can walk in the fulness of my calling and to break habits that do not serve me, and to help inspire, educate, and set others free from false financial narratives. With that said, here are some ways in which you can give each dollar you make, an assignment to work for you instead of giving it away to another person or organization that will maximize their returns and pay you little or nothing in return. Hint: This is a form of modern-day slavery or servitude especially when you're obligated by positioning, to give your money away.

Let's get to ways of diversifying your internal financial DNA and creating wealth, for your family, community, and generations to come. This list of ways to strategize, save, and invest your money or other assets, is not meant to be all encompassing nor is it deemed to be financial advice. As a financial Counselor who is only sharing from my knowledge, personal experiences, and mistakes, as well as experience working directly with people from all walks of life who just need some pivoting or support from getting where they are to where they want to be.

Cryptocurrency

The Cryptocurrency industry is still in the early stages of growth and has been preparing for mass adoption. I believe strongly that cryptocurrency is leading the way for the greatest wealth transfer man will ever see or experience again.

Digital currency on the blockchain is setting people free around the world and providing means to access where they can take a little of what they can and maximize returns by a thousand-fold in some cases. This is without even having much knowledge or insights into the industry. There is this guy I used to work with who I later spoke with during the pandemic, and he told me how while on a job he was working at for a period of time, a gentleman told him to get Doge coin when it first started attracting attention. He did not really know anything about it from his conversation with this gentleman, so he looked into it and bought a Doge coin.

A short time later, he told me how he made over $200k on that small transaction that he really knew very little about. This is where opportunity plus action reaped great rewards for him. And here's the thing, instead of holding on to the profits or keeping the coins on an exchange, he cashed out and used the funds to invest into a new property right before things started to really shoot up in the housing market.

The rise of cryptocurrency is literally setting people free and empowering them with endless possibilities to generate and create wealth, not overnight but by one transaction at a time. As with everything, you must have purpose and discipline, otherwise, your efforts become fleeting.

Precious Metals

Precious metals, rare earth metals are God's property that He has given to man to access and steward over apart from any man made structure or institution or another way of saying it, "single point of failure." These metals such as gold, silver, platinum, palladium, rhodium, and tritium are highly prized commodities that you can invest in by purchasing some of these assets with online precious metals dealers or exchanges such as kitcom.com where you can research the market and make purchases.

Others include provident metals.com, apmex.com, panthermetals.com, jmbullion.com among others. You can also become a direct investor with some companies that need to raise funds for new exploration projects, or you can also go through your brokerage such as Fidelity, SoFi (if you're a beginner and new to investing), J.P. Morgan, Webull, Merril Lynch, and Vanguard. There are more to choose from, but these platforms will allow you the opportunity to take ownership in real value investing by purchasing stock, options, or ETF's (you don't own the stock or asset but allow you to in a group of funds tied to the direct value of those assets, allowing for some diversification and risk mitigation.

Keep in mind, given our current political and geo-political climate, these assets can realize greater fluctuations and change in price. As demand increases, the value of the underlying assets can go up significantly. In fact, it is hard to find a lot of Rhodium right now and what you do find, its price is well above Gold at $6000 per ounce currently.

Here are some little-known facts, there is a network of businesses in North Carolina, Pennsylvania, New Jersey, and other states along the east coast that transact business using real bullions. The network was once much bigger but expert, Bernard von Nothaus (67 years old at the time), was arrested and placed in a jail all the way up in the Appalachian Mountains in Asheville, North Carolina after gaining traction and support for the "Liberty Dollar" he successfully and lawfully minted with over $7 million dollars of gold and silver bullion in circulation at the time of my discovery. I found out that a lot of the hardworking, law-abiding Americans, many retired seniors, had their legally purchased or bartered assets confiscated by the American Government. FBI agents raided a lot of their assets that were stored in a special warehouse.

True events like this should tell you, precious metals hold great value for exceeding that of any "fiat", at least from my research and observations and more importantly, over the course of history with the wars, conquest, and disputes over territory. This is why in 2024 and 2025, you will start hearing more about various cryptocurrencies on the blockchain being backed by real gold and silver.

(https://thewarningsigns.blogspot.com/2011/04/67-year-old-man arrested-for-minting.html)

Remember, money is not the end all. It is not your harvest. It's a seed to your harvest. Where you plant it, it will always grow. It's just a matter of whose field you are planting in each day.

High Yield Savings

This is another way to preserve and grow your dollars especially to cover for emergencies or urgent financial matters instead of borrowing a high interest loan or incurring fees which erode your purchasing power and any dollars you earned. It's another way to have your money working for you, especially considering higher inflation, increased gas prices, and rising food prices. In California you now must pay extra for bagged groceries unless you can bring your own.

Due to lower bank yields, fleeing customers, and market losses in addition to increased cost, and mitigating risk of offering new loans, banks, since the pandemic, have been encouraging people to hold their money in the banks by incentivizing them with high yield savings accounts ranging in most cases from 3.5 percent to 5.25 percent compound interest on current savings and money market accounts. This is with select financial institutions of course. They all have their pros and cons for opening and/or holding certain amounts of money to earn interest and other bonuses, like Chase bank offering $200 - $300 in cash incentives for new account holders who hold funds in those new accounts for at least 90 days. Some accounts will require you to do a certain amount of transactions within that same period of time, 90 days, in order to receive the cash bonuses for opening a new account. Do your own research and look for the current year's list of top 5 or 10 banking products with favorable returns. This is of course if you trust the banks enough to hold your money for any l

Treasury Bonds

Treasury Bonds or securities is another method of investing and preserving your assets, especially in times of volatility, holding short-term treasury bonds as a holding place to protect large sums of money when deciding where you want to invest or place your money long-term is often a safe option as well.

When I do my financial counseling, I encourage clients to explore options where they can park their money in a separate account from their regular expenses so that their money is working for them, yielding returns to continue growing what they have without the fear of loss or uncertainty. This is a great way to protect their purchasing power and the diminishing factor of long-term inflation hikes.

Depending on your choice of bonds, whether federal or municipal, how long you may need to hold the bonds, whether short-term or long-term, in addition to the current economic climate is an important consideration as well when it comes to your ability to access funds and transfer them to a new vehicle that may be more suitable.

To learn more, you can visit www[2].[3]treasurydirefct[4].gov[5].

2. http://www.treasurydirefct.gov

3. http://www.treasurydirefct.gov

4. http://www.treasurydirefct.gov

5. http://www.treasurydirefct.gov

(https://treasurydirect.gov/merketable-securities/selling-marketable securities/[6])

Other investments that may be not so common for the average person also include:

- Agriculture

- Raising Alpacas and selling them for their fur to clothing designers or other manufacturers.

- Investing in treasure hunting projects.

- Investing in wines.

- Investing in Paintings through fractional investments over time.

- Real Estate: Personal Property, Commercial Property, and Land.

- Franchises.

- Micro Loans.

- Investing in projects in Africa and more.

Whatever you ultimately decide to choose as an investment vehicle and the preservation of your assets, make sure you stay on top of the market, or things you have an expertise in, or are very passionate about. Always be learning, make calculated decisions by assessing the pros and the cons of choosing one opportunity over another. Make sure you have a strong and reliable team to work with. As the African proverb says, "If you want to go fast, go alone. If you want to go far, go together."

Lastly, do not depend on one source for an income stream, but always seek ways to viably diversify and trust your gut instincts because being able to discern rightly comes with great wisdom over time and is way more valuable than riches, gold, things, or anything else in the natural world you can accumulate.

6. https://treasurydirect.gov/merketable-securities/selling-marketable-securities

Having Purpose

Let's talk about purpose for a moment. Where and why, you invest your assets and hard earned money and the vehicles you choose for preservation and growth. It does not matter if it's gold, silver, rhodium, cryptocurrency, land, business ventures, the securities markets, etc. Before you start anything, you need to have some kind of purpose for doing what you do. You need to consider your own personal goals, needs, desires, and strategy.

When investing, know your own risk tolerance threshold because you need to know what you can handle or not handle if you experience catastrophic loss of funds or see your portfolio go from $100,000 to $5,000, are you going to panic? Will you be stressed out? These things are real because often people are influenced by two major things, fear, or greed. Both are spiritual in nature and can cause you to lose more than money. You can lose your peace of mind.

During the pandemic, some people panic or committed suicide because they watched their portfolio lose millions or hundreds or thousands of dollars in value. In other cases, people put all their assets up as leverage to borrow against, such as their home or large 401k balances, to borrow against, which usually for most people is a high-risk play. I suggest 99 percent of the people steer clear of this type of investment unless you have the resources to cover a call on an order that goes sideways, you have a very high tolerance for risk, and you are ok with the potential risk of loss involved.

In each of these above examples, fear or greed was involved but also lack of knowledge and experience were also factors as well. It is always better to keep your investments simple, be consistent, and let time work for you. You can and often will pivot along the way when it comes to investments.

Here are some tips to help guide you when you decide to invest in anything in life:

1. Have some clear goal for why you want to invest.

2. Is it to make more money?

3. Is it to grow your asset values?

4. Is it to create additional sources of income?

5. Are you trying to recoup previous losses?

6. Are you trying to set yourself up for retirement?

A. Know the risk and your responsibility to those risks before you take a leap into any investments.

1. Do you get easily stressed out or frazzled over money? 2. Do you manage money well?

3. Do you have a level of understanding about investing or growing your money?

4. Do emotions or logic dictate your actions when it comes to money or investing?

5. Do you diversify or put all your funds in one basket? B. What type of investor would you consider yourself to be?

1. High Risk Investor = Aggressive Growth or High-Income Investor. More volatility and ebbs and flows such as Option Calls, Commodities, Cryptocurrency, Futures, Direct Stock Purchases, Pink Sheet Stocks, etc.

2. Moderate Risk Investor = More balanced with less risk and guaranteed returns or more consistent returns or growth over time (Less volatile and more stable returns over time such as Mutual Funds, ETF's, silver, gold etc.

3. Moderate or extremely Moderate Investor = Risk Adverse, looking for an investment vehicle that is more stable such as CD's, Treasury Notes, Series EE Bonds, High Yield Savings, accounts, Money Market Accounts, and in some cases, insurance products if you start early enough.

No matter what, you need to understand your relationship with money and the decisions you make along the way because there will be times when things don't go as planned based on your values, and goals. When you have these two are locked in, you can make better, more informed decisions and more along the way. This also helps make pivoting and weathering market volatility and economic instability more palatable and you won't find yourself feeling overwhelmed with uncertainty.

With that said, as previously stated, always do your research, know what you have, ask questions, and stay focused on your long-term exit strategy. Lastly, below are some tips I consider before moving into a position of any kind:

1. What is my personal reason for choosing a particular investment over another?

2. What funds am I using to make this purchase?

3. Is this a lump sum investment or regular dollar cost average such as each pay period, monthly, weekly, etc.

4. What are my emotions regarding this investment?

5. Never be anxious to buy or sell any asset?

6. Is this a good time to invest my money?

7. How much can I afford to lose?

8. What do I desire long-term?

9. How is this company managed or who is running the company?

10. How do you do your research?

11. Do you have alerts and triggers set?

12. Does this investment yield consistent gains over time? 13. Is this a stable growth investment or short-term play?

Here are some of my tops picks when it comes to cryptocurrencies with solid, real world use cases:

1. XRP – Quick, cost efficient, and low carbo footprint. Digital Gold.

2. XLM – Fast transactions, transfer millions of dollars with an average transaction cost of .000002 XLM will empower millions of people to send and receive funds quickly across the globe.

3. Cardano – Open Source, focuses on security, and scalability and is designed for easy scalability for municipalities and growing enterprises around the world.

4. Solana – decentralized Finance platform that uses Proof-of Stake (POS) and Proof-of History (POH) to verify the previous transactions, offers low fees, and will process

transaction seconds.

5. VeChain – Major partnerships with international firms, secure, and allows companies worldwide to track, secure and protect inventory from being stolen, verifies inventory, and has a low carbon footprint.

6. Chainlink – Allows for many smart contracts by allowing for "off-chain" data to be integrated into the network. It has a large "open source" community.

7. Polygon – Designed to allow for Ethereum based blockchain projects to be built on top of and scaled securely and with lower fees. It is a rapidly growing ecosystem, it supports multiple application types for developers, enterprises, and more.

8. Kaspa – Does not orphan blocks but allows them to still exist on the blockchain, has high block rates without compromising security, it currently does 1 block per second with a future goal of 100 blocks per second.

9. XDC - I consider this like platinum, for the simple fact, it offers public and private security levels while also offering security. It provides interoperability for large municipalities, offers KYC nodes, and financial institutions with 2000 TPS (Transactions Per Second), it's compatible with EVM

(Ethereum Virtual Machines) and smart contracts. It is a deployable layer 2 asset and has an international footprint. 10. IoTex – Has an ecosystem powered by devices on the network, it is decentralized for the privacy and security of each product user, with a team of more than 40 engineers and research scientists. They have their own EVM compatible machine. Each user device is considered self-sovereign.

11. Gala – Funded by top gaming developers. Gamers have freedom and control. It has attractive games and excellent UX design. Created with a "games-first" methodology. As an up-and-coming Web-3 blockchain, Gala Games is creating an experience where gamers can play, earn, and own content. The gamers on the blockchain can seamlessly trade peer-to-peer. Gala has current projects with Dreamworks, AMC, and Will Wright who is the creator of "The Sims."

12. Sandbox – Creates a unique gaming experience with amazing graphics on an "play-to-earn_ model, incentivizes adopters of the blockchain as both gamer and creator. Some

users have earned enough Sand tokens to pay their monthly rent.

13. BitTorrent – Decentralized, peer-to-peer, file sharing blockchain that allows users from around the world to share all types of content fast and privately such as videos, music, files, documents, and more. BitTorrent now offers VPN and ad-free browsing.

14. DigiByte - Offers high level, military grade security, using 5 algorithms, it is free, and open source. It was forked from Bitcoin initially. It has 3 layers, smart contract, public ledger, nodes for relay transactions. They have a great community that is willing to support and promote other projects.

There are many other amazing great blockchain projects doing amazing things and even on the verge of new breakthroughs. Too many to count or talk about. This list I provided is just a few of the key ones that stand out on the market today.

Real Crypto News

With a few major conglomerates controlling most of the news along with many other companies in different sectors of the American society, it has become apparent and vitally important for you to validate where you source your news and information, particularly select individuals either trying to discount cryptocurrency as a whole or trying to stir you towards one main cryptocurrency, Bitcoin. This is very dangerous and can cause many people to experience shock in the near future due to a rug pulled by the same market makers in stocks also being the ones to manipulate and influence the crypto market, better known as well.

Many of the people in the media telling retail investors what they should or should not do with their money, do not have your best interest in mind. If they did, they would stop talking in code, dancing around questions when asked yes? Or No? I believe you should be listening to certain social media influencers online while still picking up queues from what is not said but alluded to when people with key market insights are talking.

With that said, never listen to the first things you hear on the news. Media is used to engage, influence, and direct the behavior of the masses throughout the country. There is a psychology behind all media outlets. The root word for media in Greek is Mda, meaning to plan or scheme. Why would any outlet that should be based on truth and unbiased facts, operate under the predisposed position to plan, or scheme. People in America have become quite divided and in fear of others based on what media pre-plans to report on.

Read Between the Lines

With all the confusion, miss information, false narratives, suggestive contents, and institutional control in high places, you must use discernment and prudence to assess the truth which will set you free mentally, financially, and socially. My desire for writing this book is to help educate you, equip you, and give you the assurance you need, to know, that you, me, and all of us every day working- and middle-class people, can and will be set free from all the lies, deceit, manipulations, bondage, death grips (mortgage loan), and indentured servitude. In fact, do you know that Mort (death) and gage (grip) is another form of binding many people to long-term debt?

Many people never pay off their mortgage and pass that debt along to their families or even lose the home they have been living in for 30 – 40 years due to needing to refinance and taking on a 2nd and even 3rd

mortgage notes which are liens or additional death grips. There are a lot of lines being cast at each of us every day and if we are not careful, just like a fish in the waters, we can easily get caught unawares where we will then be cast into the net with the rest of society.

"Life Does Not Consist in the Abundance of Things"

As we near the conclusion of these last few pages of insights, understanding the meaning and reason behind everything you do, it is important to know what your reasoning is for going into crypto? What do you hope to gain from investing? I am not talking about things tangible but what is intrinsic and valuable to you and your family. Oftentimes in America, people do things because that's what's proper, or it does not disrupt the status quote.

Many people are influenced by what they are told even though they may not know the real meaning of the Why? Many are heavily influenced by marketing and advertising, images, and sounds.

Everyday people are bombarded, being influenced, and manipulated into what others want them to do. In an article written by Aaron O'Neill, June 21, 2022 which can be found at www[7].[8]statista[9].com/statistics/10/0/69/black-and-slave-population-us-1790-1880/[10].

There were roughly 700k slaves recorded by 1790 or 18 percent of the American population. In 1860, prior to the Civil War, there were 4 million slaves. Now let's bring that to today. If slavery was about building agriculture and having a sustainable work force at the lowest cost basis possible, though, albeit, nefarious and deplorable and inexcusable means, what do you think we have today? We have a disproportionate number of people in America alone, that are literally in slavery or indentured servitude. Why? Because most of us were taught to believe in a system that was not designed by us but made for us.

People are being told to go out and buy things and be sold on things they don't need, can't afford, or not quite ready for. This is why it is so important to have a value system that is not dependent upon or contingent upon things or anyone else's system they say you should follow. Life has never consisted in the abundance of things, and everyone cannot handle or even need a lot of money or things to live well. Happy, and whole lives that are truly abundant.

Today in America, more people are sick, stressed out, unhappy, depressed, and oppressed like never before and this is all because of messaging and programming through movies, television, our schools, music, and commercials everywhere you go. Out of an hour of television watching, about 30 minutes or more is nothing but ridiculous commercials and suggestive advertising.

7.

http://www.statista.com/statistics/10/0/69/black-and-slave-population-us-1790-1880 8.
http://www.statista.com/statistics/10/0/69/black-and-slave-population-us-1790-1880 9.
http://www.statista.com/statistics/10/0/69/black-and-slave-population-us-1790-1880 10.
http://www.statista.com/statistics/10/0/69/black-and-slave-population-us-1790-1880

When you have your own goals and a clear purpose for your life, then everything you do in life has real meaning and is connected to an intended outcome for the betterment of yourself, your family, and your community, and the world at large. Good intentions will produce life and bad intentions will produce death and prove to be futile in the end.

So, I pose this question to you, if you become a multi-millionaire today through investing in cryptocurrency or some other means by which you become financially free from this current burdensome fiat system and you were able to eradicate all your debts, what would you do with the money and abundance you have remaining in your possession? No one can answer this question for you but you. God Himself will not even force you to do what He has called you to do because it is your responsibility. Israel's first King, Saul, made a choice even though he knew the task he was given to do but how he went about things ultimately cost him and his sons everything.

It is not wealth and riches that makes life better, it is what's in your heart and your decisions that ultimately determine your happiness and success. Consider this, if you are double minded or become indecisive about how you handle the provision within your possession, someone else is already in position and will willingly, without hesitation, siphon away what you do have. But when you have a strong conviction and a clearly established value system, you will know exactly what to do to preserve, resource, and care for others in need and for the greater good of the community around you.

You can be debt free without having a deficit mindset while freely giving to others and not becoming consumed by the things you have. Do not let man tell you what you can or can't have or what you are capable of regardless of what you are in life. I refute the phrase that, "you will own nothing and be happy," as penned in a 2016 WEF essay by Danish politician, Ida Auken. This may be his narrative, but it does not have to be yours. You can own what you desire and be happy too!

Doing Do Diligence

As you already know, there is a lot of information out there and a lot of it designed to bring confusion or to capture your attention to get you to buy something, even when it comes to accessing information which can be often overwhelming, confusing, and time consuming. That is why I have provided a list of resources, tools, and content below to help you on your search for insights, veritas, and direction. The following resources are not intended to be all inclusive or a recommendation of what you should or should not do. These are simply some of the resources and people I have found to be helpful and beneficial along my own journey when it comes to learning and researching about cryptocurrency, precious metals, investments, and all things money.

Financial Tools and Resources

Investopedia.com

Federalreserve.gov

Wallethub.com

Money.com

Clark.com

Studentaid.gov

Kitco.com

Wikipedia.org

Jmbullion.com

Coinmarketcap.com

YouTube.com

Trusted YouTube Influencer

The Economic Ninja

Ben Hedges

Cryptos R Us

Jame Gordon Crypto

Ask Sebby

Paul Barron Network

The Bearable Bull

Meet Kevin

The Diary of A CEO

Raul Pal

Michael Saylor

Lynette Zang

Robert Kiyosaki

The Elite Fear Podcast

There are many people and resources to research and follow but these are just a few of the channels. I have come across this in my research. A big part of research for me comes down to listening to key information a person is sharing with me, observation, what was not said or left out, and asking questions to get to what? Where? Why? And even How?

These questions always help me to dig deeper and get to the root of what I am looking for and gain enough understanding to continue each stage of learning. This was the case when I mentioned about the gentleman who told me about his friend trying to get him involved in cryptocurrency but he never took it seriously.

At the end of our conversation, my interest was piqued enough to where I said, I must do something about this because I want to understand what cryptocurrency is and how it works, and how I can get involved. I initially started slow. Things picked up once I realized how things really worked in this market but nevertheless, I showed up!

Only The Beginning

As we conclude, I want to thank you for taking the time to purchase, download, or listen to the podcast version of this book. This book represents a part of my journey with money and cryptocurrency and some of the lessons I have learned along the way. This journey started over 3 ½ years ago for me and did not start making more sense until about 2 years ago as I began understanding some of the terminology, trends, and insights into blockchain versus cryptocurrency and the habits and characteristics of how the industry moves and responds to news and anticipated rumors, and updates, along with historical indications some have shared.

My hope is that everything I have shared and the conclusions I have come to, will make it easier for you to learn, grow, and understand how to navigate the cryptocurrency industry and money as a form of currency and transacting commerce. The possibility of what blockchain technology has opened up to every man, woman, and child across the world, are endless. Dream Big, Think Big, and be ever relentless in your pursuit for more without compromising who you are. Here's to the revolution of making all things new!

Don't miss out!

Visit the website below and you can sign up to receive emails whenever John Savage publishes a new book. There's no charge and no obligation.

https://books2read.com/r/B-A-LDHEB-FYVYC

BOOKS2READ

Connecting independent readers to independent writers.